© Copyright 2022 - All rights reserved.
The content contained within this book may not be reproduced, duplicated, or transmitted without direct written permission from the author or the publisher.

Under no circumstances will any blame or legal responsibility be held against the publisher, or author, for any damages, reparation, or monetary loss due to the information contained within this book, either directly or indirectly.

Legal Notice:
This book is copyright protected. It is only for personal use. You cannot amend, distribute, sell, use, quote or paraphrase any part, or the content within this book, without the consent of the author or publisher.

Disclaimer Notice:
Please note the information contained within this document is for educational and entertainment purposes only. All effort has been executed to present accurate, up to date, reliable, complete information. No warranties of any kind are declared or implied. Readers acknowledge that the author is not engaged in the rendering of legal, financial, medical, or professional advice. The content within this book has been derived from various sources. Please consult a licensed professional before attempting any techniques outlined in this book.

By reading this document, the reader agrees that under no circumstances is the author responsible for any losses, direct or indirect, that are incurred as a result of the use of the information contained within this document, including, but not limited to, errors, omissions, or inaccuracies.

# Contents

- We Wish You A Merry Christmas..................................................4
- Jingle Bells..................................................................5-6
- Rudolph The Red-Nosed Reindeer..................................7
- Frosty The Snowman...................................................8-9
- Santa Claus Is Coming To Town....................................10
- Silent Night....................................................................11
- The Twelve Days Of Christmas.................................12-14
- All I Want For Christmas Is My Two Front Teeth.........15
- Away In A Manger........................................................16
- Rockin' Around The Christmas Tree.............................17
- I Saw Mommy Kissing Santa Clause.............................18
- It's beginning To Look A Lot Like Christmas.................19
- Let It Snow!...................................................................20

# Contents

White Christmas .................................................................... 21

Have Yourself A Merry Little Christmas ........................ 22

It's The Most Wonderful Time Of The Year ................ 23-24

A Holly Jolly Christmas ..................................................... 25

Jingle Bell Rock .................................................................... 26-27

Here Comes Santa Claus ................................................... 28-29

Merry Christmas Everybody ............................................ 30-31

Feliz Navidad ....................................................................... 32-33

O Holy Night ........................................................................ 34

The First Noel ...................................................................... 35-36

Joy To The World ............................................................... 37

Last Christmas .................................................................... 38-39

# We Wish You A Merry Christmas

*Written and Composed by*
*Arthur Warrell*
*In 1939*

We wish you a merry Christmas
We wish you a merry Christmas
We wish you a merry Christmas
And a happy New Year

[Chorus]
Good tidings we bring to you and your kin
We wish a merry Christmas and a happy New Year

[Chorus]
Good tidings we bring to you and your kin
We wish you a merry Christmas and a happy New Year
For we all like our figgy pudding
For we all like our figgy pudding
For we all like our figgy pudding
With all this good cheer
[Chorus]
Good tidings we bring to you and your kin
We wish you a merry Christmas and a happy New Year
And we won't go until we get some
And we won't go until we get some
And we won't go until we get some
So bring some out here
[Chorus]
Good tidings we bring to you and your kin
We wish you a merry Christmas and a happy New Year
We wish you a merry Christmas
We wish you a merry Christmas
We wish you a merry Christmas
And a happy New Year

# Jingle Bells

*Written and Composed by
James Lord Pierpont
In 1857*

Dashing through the snow
In a one-horse open sleigh
O'er the fields we go
Laughing all the way
Bells on bobtails ring
Making spirits bright
What fun it is to ride and sing
A sleighing song tonight, oh!

Jingle bells, jingle bells
Jingle all the way
Oh, what fun it is to ride
In a one-horse open sleigh, hey!
Jingle bells, jingle bells
Jingle all the way
Oh what fun it is to ride
In a one-horse open sleigh

Now the ground is white
Go it while you're young
Take the girls tonight
Sing this sleighing song
Get a bobtailed bay
Two forty for his speed
And hitch him to an open sleigh
And you will take the lead

(Continues on next page)

Oh, jingle bells, jingle bells
Jingle all the way
Oh, what fun it is to ride
In a one-horse open sleigh, hey!
Jingle bells, jingle bells
Jingle all the way
Oh, what fun it is to ride
In a one-horse open sleigh
Oh, what fun it is to ride
In one horse open sleigh!

# Rudolph The Red-Nosed Reindeer

*Written and Composed by*
*Johnny Marks*
*In 1939*

You know Dasher and Dancer and Prancer and Vixen
Comet and Cupid and Donner and Blitzen
But do you recall
The most famous reindeer of all?

Rudolph the Red-Nosed Reindeer
Had a very shiny nose
And if you ever saw it
You would even say it glows

All of the other reindeer
Used to laugh and call him names
They never let poor Rudolph
Join in any reindeer games

Then one foggy Christmas Eve
Santa came to say
"Rudolph, with your nose so bright
Won't you guide my sleigh tonight?"

Then how the reindeer loved him
As they shouted out with glee
"Rudolph the Red-Nosed Reindeer
You'll go down in history"

# Frosty The Snowman

*Written and Composed by*
*Walter E. Rollins, Steve Nelson and Gene Autry*
*In 1950*

Frosty the Snowman
Was a jolly happy soul
With a corn cob pipe and a button nose
And two eyes made out of coal#

Frosty the Snowman
Is a fairytale they say
He was made of snow, but the children know
How he came to life one day

There must have been some magic
In that old top hat they found
For when they placed it on his head
He began to dance around

Oh, Frosty the Snowman
Was alive as he could be
And the children say he could laugh and play
Just the same as you and me

Frosty the Snowman
Was a jolly happy soul
With a corn cob pipe and a button nose
And two eyes made out of coal

Frosty the Snowman
A fairytale they say
Was made of snow
But he came to life one day

(Continues on next page)

There must have been some magic
In that old top hat they found (some magic in that hat)
For when they placed it on his head
He began to dance around

Frosty the Snowman (snowman)
Knew the sun was hot that day (hot that day)
So he said, "Let's run, and we'll have some fun
Now before I melt away"

Frosty the Snowman
Had to hurry on his way
But he waved good-bye, saying, "Don't you cry
I'll be back again some day!"

# Santa Claus Is Coming To Town

*Written and Composed by*
*Haven Gillespie and J. Fred Coots*
*In 1934*

You better watch out, you better not cry
You better not pout, I'm tellin' you why
Santa Claus is comin' to town

He's makin' a list and checkin' it twice
He's gonna find out who's naughty, and nice
Santa Claus is comin' to town

He sees you when you're sleepin'
He knows when you're awake
He knows if you've been bad or good
So be good, for goodness' sake

You better watch out, you better not cry
You better not pout, I'm tellin' you why
Santa Claus is comin' to town

With little tin horns and little toy drums
Rooty toot-toots and rummy tum-tums
Santa Claus is comin' to town

And curly head dolls that toddle and coo
Elephants, boats, and kiddie cars too
Santa Claus is comin' to town

The kids in Girl and Boy land
Will have a jubilee
They're gonna build a Toyland town
All around the Christmas tree

You better watch out, better not cry
You better not pout, I'm tellin' you why
Santa Claus is comin' to town
There he is, to town

# Silent Night

*Written and Composed by*
*Franz Xaver Gruber and Joseph Mohr*
*In 1818*

Silent night, holy night!
All is calm, all is bright.
Round yon Virgin, Mother and Child.
Holy infant so tender and mild,
Sleep in heavenly peace,
Sleep in heavenly peace

Silent night, holy night!
Shepherds quake at the sight.
Glories stream from heaven afar
Heavenly hosts sing Alleluia,
Christ the Savior is born!
Christ the Savior is born

Silent night, holy night!
Son of God love's pure light.
Radiant beams from Thy holy face
With dawn of redeeming grace,
Jesus Lord, at Thy birth
Jesus Lord, at Thy birth

# The Twelve Days Of Christmas

*Written and Composed by*
*Frederic Austin and Andrew Carter*
*In 1909*

On the first day of Christmas, my true love sent to me
A partridge in a pear tree

On the second day of Christmas, my true love sent to me
Two turtle doves
And a partridge in a pear tree

On the third day of Christmas, my true love sent to me
Three French hens
Two turtle doves

On the forth day of Christmas, my true love sent to me
Four calling birds
Three French hens
Two turtle doves
And a partridge in a pear tree

On the fifth day of Christmas, my true love sent to me
Five golden rings
Four calling birds
Three French hens
Two turtle doves
And a partridge in a pear tree

On the sixth day of Christmas, my true love sent to me
Six geese a-laying
Five golden rings
Four calling birds
Three French hens
Two turtle doves
And a partridge in a pear tree

(Continues on next page)

On the seventh day of Christmas, my true love sent to me
Seven swans a-swimming
Six geese a-laying
Five golden rings
Four calling birds
Three French hens
Two turtle doves
And a partridge in a pear tree

On the eighth day of Christmas, my true love sent to me
Eight maids a-milking
Seven swans a-swimming
Six geese a-laying
Five golden rings
Four calling birds
Three French hens
Two turtle doves
And a partridge in a pear tree

On the ninth day of Christmas, my true love sent to me
Nine ladies dancing
Eight maids a-milking
Seven swans a-swimming
Six geese a-laying
Five golden rings
Four calling birds
Three French hens
Two turtle doves
And a partridge in a pear tree

(Continues on next page)

On the tenth day of Christmas, my true love sent to me
Ten lords a-leaping
Nine ladies dancing
Eight maids a-milking
Seven swans a-swimming
Six geese a-laying
Five golden rings
Four calling birds
Three French hens
Two turtle doves
And a partridge in a pear tree

On the eleventh day of Christmas, my true love sent to me
Eleven pipers piping
Ten lords a-leaping
Nine ladies dancing
Eight maids a-milking
Seven swans a-swimming
Six geese a-laying
Five golden rings
Four calling birds
Three French hens
Two turtle doves
And a partridge in a pear tree

On the twelve day of Christmas, my true love sent to me
Twelve drummers drumming
Eleven pipers piping
Ten lords a-leaping
Nine ladies dancing
Eight maids a-milking
Seven swans a-swimming
Six geese a-laying
Five golden rings
Four calling birds
Three French hens
Two turtle doves
And a partridge in a pear tree

# All I Want For Christmas Is My Two Front Teeth

*Written and Composed by*
*Donald Yetter Gardner*
*In 1944*

Everybody stops and stares at me
These two teeth are gone as you can see
I don't know just who to blame for this catastrophe
But my one wish on Christmas Eve is as plain as can be

All I want for Christmas is my two front teeth
My two front teeth
See my two front teeth
Gee, if I could only have my two front teeth
Then I could wish you, "Merry Christmas"

It seems so long since I could say
"Sister, Susie sitting on a thistle!"
Gosh, oh gee, how happy I'd be, if I could only whistle

All I want for Christmas is my two front teeth
My two front teeth
See my two front teeth
Gee, if I could only have my two front teeth
Then I could wish you, "Merry Christmas"

It seems so long since I could say
"Sister, Susie sitting on a thistle!"
Gosh, oh gee, how happy I'd be, if I could only whistle

All I want for Christmas is my two front teeth
My two front teeth
See my two front teeth
Gee, if I could only have my two front teeth
Then I could wish you, "Merry Christmas"

# Away In A Manger

*Written and Composed by
William J. Kirkpatrick and James R. Murray
In 1882*

Away in a manger
No crib for a bed
The little Lord Jesus
Laid down his sweet head
The stars in the bright sky
Looked down where he lay
The little Lord Jesus
Asleep on the hay

The cattle are lowing
The baby awakes
But little Lord Jesus
No crying he makes
I love thee, Lord Jesus
Look down from the sky
And stay by my side
Until morning is nigh

Be near me, Lord Jesus
I ask you to stay
Close by me forever
And love me I pray
Bless all the dear children
In thy tender care
And take us for heaven
To live with thee there

# Rockin' Around The Christmas Tree

*Written and Composed by*
*Johnny Marks*
*In 1958*

Rockin' around the Christmas tree
At the Christmas party hop
Mistletoe hung where you can see
Every couple tries to stop

Rockin' around the Christmas tree
Let the Christmas spirit ring
Later we'll have some pumpkin pie
And we'll do some carolling

You will get a sentimental feeling
When you hear
Voices singing let's be jolly
Deck the halls with boughs of holly

Rockin' around the Christmas tree
Have a happy holiday
Everyone dancing merrily
In the new old-fashioned way

You will get a sentimental feeling
When you hear
Voices singing let's be jolly
Deck the halls with boughs of holly

Rockin' around the Christmas tree
Have a happy holiday
Everyone dancing merrily
In the new old fashioned way

# I Saw Mommy Kissing Santa Claus

*Written and Composed by*
*Tommie Connor*
*In 1952*

Wow! Mommy's kissing Santa Claus!

I saw Mommy kissing Santa Claus (kissing, kissing Santa Claus)
Underneath the mistletoe last night
She didn't see me creep
Down the stairs to have a peep
She thought that I was tucked up
In my bedroom, fast asleep

Then I saw Mommy tickle Santa Claus (tickle, tickle, Santa Claus)
Underneath his beard so snowy white
Oh, what a laugh it would have been
If daddy had only seen
Mommy kissing Santa Claus last night

He saw Mommy kissing (kissing, kissing) Santa Claus
I did! I really did see Mommy kissing Santa Claus
And I'm gonna tell my dad

Then I saw Mommy tickle Santa Claus (tickle, tickle Santa Claus)
Underneath his beard so snowy white
Oh, what a laugh it would have been
If daddy had only seen
Mommy kissing Santa Claus last night

Oh, what a laugh it would have been
If daddy had only seen
Mommy kissing Santa Claus last night

I did! I did! I really did see Mommy kissing Santa Claus
You gotta believe me! You just gotta believe me!
Come on, fellas, believe me!
You just gotta believe me!
Come on, you gotta believe me!

# It's Beginning To Look A Lot Like Christmas

*Written and composed by*
*Meredith Willson*
*In 1951*

It's beginning to look a lot like Christmas
Everywhere you go;
Take a look at the five and ten
It's glistening once again
With candy canes and silver lanes aglow.

It's beginning to look a lot like Christmas
Toys in every store
But the prettiest sight to see is the holly that will be
On your own front door.

A pair of hopalong boots and a pistol that shoots
Is the wish of Barney and Ben;
Dolls that will talk and will go for a walk
Is the hope of Janice and Jen;
And Mom and Dad can hardly wait for school to start again.

It's beginning to look a lot like Christmas
Everywhere you go;
There's a tree in the Grand Hotel, one in the park as well,
It's the sturdy kind that doesn't mind the snow.

It's beginning to look a lot like Christmas;
Soon the bells will start,
And the thing that will make them ring is the carol that you sing
Right within your heart

It's beginning to look a lot like Christmas
Toys in every store
But the prettiest sight to see is the holly that will be
On your own front door.

Sure it's Christmas once more...

# Let It Snow

*Written and Composed by
Jule Styne and Sammy Cahn
In 1945*

Oh, the weather outside is frightful
But the fire is so delightful
And since we've no place to go
Let it snow, let it snow, let it snow

Man, it doesn't show signs of stopping
And I've brought me some corn for popping
The lights are turned way down low
Let it snow, let it snow

When we finally kiss good-night
How I'll hate going out in the storm
But if you really hold me tight
All the way home I'll be warm

And the fire is slowly dying
And, my dear, we're still goodbying
But as long as you love me so
Let it snow, let it snow and snow

When we finally kiss good-night
How I'll hate going out in the storm
But if you really grab me tight
All the way home I'll be warm

Oh, the fire is slowly dying
And, my dear, we're still goodbying
But as long as you love me so
Let it snow, let it snow, let it snow

# White Christmas

*Written and Composed by
Irving Berlin
In 1942*

I'm dreaming of a white Christmas
Just like the ones I used to know
Where the tree tops glisten
And children listen
To hear sleigh bells in the snow

I'm dreaming of a white Christmas
With every Christmas card I write
May your days be merry and bright
And may all your Christmases be white

I'm dreaming of a white Christmas
Just like the ones I used to know
Where the tree tops glisten
And children listen
To hear sleigh bells in the snow

I'm dreaming of a white Christmas
With every Christmas card I write
May your days be merry and bright
And may all your Christmases
May all your Christmases be white

# Have Yourself A Merry Little Christmas

*Written and Composed by
Hugh Martin and Ralph Blane
In 1943*

Have yourself a merry little Christmas
Let your heart be light
From now on our troubles
Will be out of sight

Have yourself a merry little Christmas
Make the Yuletide gay
From now on our troubles
Will be miles away, oh ooh

Here we are as in olden days
Happy golden days of yore, ah
Faithful friends who are dear to us
Gather near to us, once more, ooh

Through the years we all will be together
If the fates allow
Hang a shining star upon the highest bough
And have yourself a merry little Christmas now

Here we are as in olden days
Happy golden days of yore
Faithful friends who are dear to us
Gather near to us, once more

Through the years we all will be together
If the fates allow
Hang a shining star upon the highest bough, oh
And have yourself a merry little Christmas now, ooh

Merry Christmas
Merry Christmas

# It's The Most Wonderful Time Of The Year

*Written and Composed by*
*Edward Pola and George Wyle*
*In 1963*

It's the most wonderful time of the year
With the kids jingle belling
And everyone telling you "be of good cheer"
It's the most wonderful time of the year

It's the hap-happiest season of all
With those holiday greetings
And gay happy meetings when friends come to call
It's the hap-happiest season of all

There'll be parties for hosting
Marshmallows for toasting
And caroling out in the snow
There'll be scary ghost stories
And tales of the glories
Of Christmases long, long ago

It's the most wonderful time of the year
There'll be much mistletoeing
And hearts will be glowing when loved ones are near
It's the most wonderful time of the year

There'll be parties for hosting
Marshmallows for toasting
And caroling out in the snow
There'll be scary ghost stories
And tales of the glories
Of Christmases long, long ago

(Continues on next page)

It's the most wonderful time of the year
There'll be much mistletoeing
And hearts will be glowing when loved ones are near
It's the most wonderful time
Yes, the most wonderful time
Oh, the most wonderful time
Of the year

# A Holly Jolly Christmas

*Written and Composed by*
*Johnny Marks*
*In 1962*

Have a holly jolly Christmas
It's the best time of the year
I don't know if there'll be snow
But have a cup of cheer

Have a holly jolly Christmas
And when you walk down the street
Say hello to friends you know
And everyone you meet

Oh ho, the mistletoe
Hung where you can see
Somebody waits for you
Kiss her once for me

Have a holly jolly Christmas
And in case you didn't hear
Oh, by golly, have a holly jolly Christmas this year

Have a holly jolly Christmas
It's the best time of the year

Have a holly jolly Christmas
And when you walk down the street
Say hello to friends you know
And everyone you meet

Oh ho, the mistletoe
Hung where you can see
Somebody waits for you
Kiss her once for me

Have a holly jolly Christmas
And in case you didn't hear
Oh, by golly, have a holly jolly Christmas this year

# Jingle Bell Rock

*Written and Composed by
Joseph Carleton Beal and James Ross Boothe
In 1957*

Jingle bell, jingle bell, jingle bell rock
Jingle bells swing and jingle bells ring
Snowin' and blowin' up bushels of fun
Now the jingle hop has begun

Jingle bell, jingle bell, jingle bell rock
Jingle bells chime in jingle bell time
Dancin' and prancin' in Jingle Bell Square
In the frosty air

What a bright time, it's the right time
To rock the night away
Jingle bell time is a swell time
To go glidin' in a one-horse sleigh

Giddy-up jingle horse, pick up your feet
Jingle around the clock
Mix and a-mingle in the jinglin' feet
That's the jingle bell rock

Jingle bell, jingle bell, jingle bell rock
Jingle bell chime in jingle bell time
Dancin' and prancin' in Jingle Bell Square
In the frosty air

What a bright time, it's the right time
To rock the night away
Jingle bell time is a swell time
To go glidin' in a one-horse sleigh

(Continues on next page)

Giddy-up jingle horse, pick up your feet
Jingle around the clock
Mix and a-mingle in the jinglin' feet
That's the jingle bell
That's the jingle bell
That's the jingle bell rock

# Here Comes Santa Claus

*Written and Composed by
Oakley Haldeman and Gene Autry
In 1947*

Here comes Santa Claus, here comes Santa Claus
Right down Santa Claus Lane
Vixen and Blitzen and all his reindeer's
Pulling on the reins
Bells are ringing, children singing
All is merry and bright
So hang your stockings and say your prayers
'Cause Santa Claus comes tonight

Here comes Santa Claus, here comes Santa Claus
Right down Santa Claus Lane
He's got a bag that's filled with toys
For boys and girls again
Hear those sleigh bells jingle-jangle
Oh, what a beautiful sight
So jump in bed and cover your head
'Cause Santa Claus comes tonight

Here comes Santa Claus, here comes Santa Claus
Right down Santa Claus Lane
He doesn't care if you're rich or poor
He loves you just the same
Santa Claus knows we're all God's children
That makes everything right
So fill your hearts with Christmas cheer
'Cause Santa Claus comes tonight

(continues on next page)

Here comes Santa Claus, here comes Santa Claus
Right down Santa Claus Lane
He'll come around when chimes ring out
That it's Christmas morn' again
Peace on Earth will come to all
If we just follow the light
So let's give thanks to the lord above
'Cause Santa Claus comes tonight

Here comes Santa Claus, here comes Santa Claus
Right down Santa Claus Lane
Vixen and Blitzen and all his reindeer's
Pulling on the reins
Bells are ringing, children singing
All is merry and bright
Hang your stockings and say your prayers
'Cause Santa Claus comes tonight!

# Merry Christmas Everybody

*Written and Composed by
Noddy Holder and Jim Lea
In 1973*

Are you hanging up a stocking on your wall?
It's the time that every Santa has a ball
Does he ride a red-nosed reindeer?
Does he turn up on his sleigh?
Do the fairies keep him sober for a day?

So here it is, Merry Christmas
Everybody's having fun
Look to the future now
It's only just begun

Are you waiting for the family to arrive?
Are you sure you've got the room to spare inside?
Does your granny always tell you
That the old songs are the best?
Then she's up and rock-'n'-rolling with the rest

So here it is, Merry Christmas
Everybody's having fun
Look to the future now
It's only just begun

What will your daddy do when he sees your momma kissing Santa Claus?

Are you hanging up a stocking on your wall?
Are you hoping that the snow will start to fall?
Do you ride on down the hillside
In a buggy you have made?
When you land upon your head then you've been slayed

(Continues on next page)

So here it is, Merry Christmas
Everybody's having fun
Look to the future now
It's only just begun

So here it is, Merry Christmas
Everybody's having fun
Look to the future now
It's only just begun

# Feliz Navidad

*Written and Composed by
Jose' Feliciano
In 1970*

Feliz navidad
Feliz navidad
Feliz navidad, prospero año y felicidad

Feliz navidad
Feliz navidad
Feliz navidad, prospero año y felicidad

I want to wish you a merry Christmas
I want to wish you a merry Christmas
I want to wish you a merry Christmas from the bottom of my heart

I want to wish you a merry Christmas
I want to wish you a merry Christmas
I want to wish you a merry Christmas from the bottom of my heart

Feliz navidad
Feliz navidad
Feliz navidad, prospero año y felicidad
A-ha!

Feliz navidad
Feliz navidad
Feliz navidad, prospero año y felicidad

I want to wish you a merry Christmas
I want to wish you a merry Christmas
I want to wish you a merry Christmas from the bottom of my heart

(continues on next page)

I want to wish you a merry Christmas
I want to wish you a merry Christmas
I want to wish you a merry Christmas from the bottom of my heart

Feliz navidad
Feliz navidad
Feliz navidad, prospero año y felicidad

Feliz navidad
Feliz navidad
Feliz navidad, prospero año y felicidad

I want to wish you a merry Christmas
I want to wish you a merry Christmas
I want to wish you a merry Christmas from the bottom of my heart

I want to wish you a merry Christmas
I want to wish you a merry Christmas
I want to wish you a merry Christmas from the bottom of my heart

Feliz navidad
Feliz navidad
Feliz navidad, prospero año y felicidad

# O Holy Night

*Written and Composed by*
*Adolphe Adam*
*In 1843*

Oh, holy night, the stars are brightly shining
It is the night of our dear Savior's birth
Long lay the world in sin and error pining
'Til He appeared and the soul felt its worth

A thrill of hope, the weary world rejoices
For yonder breaks a new and glorious morn'
Fall on your knees, oh, hear the angels' voices
Oh, night divine, oh, night when Christ was born
Oh, night divine, oh, night, oh night divine

A thrill of hope, the weary world rejoices
For yonder breaks a new and glorious morn'
Fall on your knees, oh, hear, hear the angels' voices
Oh, night divine, yeah, oh, night when Christ was born
Oh, night divine, oh night divine

Oh, night divine
It is the night when Christ was born
Oh, night divine
Oh, night divine
Oh, night divine holy night

# The First Noel

*Written and Composed by
William B. Sandys and Davies Gilbert
In 1823*

The First Noel the Angels did say
Was to certain poor shepherds in fields as they lay
In fields where they lay keeping their sheep
On a cold winter's night that was so deep
Noel, Noel, Noel, Noel
Born is the King of Israel!

They looked up and saw a star
Shining in the East beyond them far
And to the earth it gave great light
And so it continued both day and night
Noel, Noel, Noel, Noel
Born is the King of Israel!

And, by the light of that same star
Three wise men came from country far
To seek for a King was their intent
And to follow the star wherever it went
Noel, Noel, Noel, Noel
Born is the King of Israel!

This star drew nigh to the northwest
O'er Bethlehem it took its rest
And there it did both stop and stay
Right over the place where Jesus lay
Noel, Noel, Noel, Noel
Born is the King of Israel!

(continues on next page)

Then entered in those Wise Men three
Fell reverently upon their knee
And offered there in his presence
Their gold and myrrh and frankincense
Noel, Noel, Noel, Noel
Born is the King of Israel!

Then let us all with one accord
Sing praises to our heavenly Lord
That hath made heaven and earth of nought
And with his blood mankind hath bought

Noel, Noel, Noel, Noel
Born is the King of Israel!

# Joy To The World

*Written and Composed by*
*Lowell Mason*
*In 1848*

Joy to the World, the Lord has come!
Let earth receive her King;
Let every heart prepare Him room,
And Heaven and nature sing,
And Heaven and nature sing,
And Heaven, and Heaven, and nature sing.

Joy to the World, the Savior reigns!
Let men their songs employ;
While fields and floods, rocks, hills and plains
Repeat the sounding joy,
Repeat the sounding joy,
Repeat, repeat, the sounding joy.

He rules the world with truth and grace,
And makes the nations prove
The glories of His righteousness,
And wonders of His love,
And wonders of His love,
And wonders, wonders, of His love.

Joy to the World, the Lord has come!
Let earth receive her King;
Let every heart prepare Him room,
And Heaven and nature sing,
And Heaven and nature sing,
And Heaven, and Heaven, and nature sing.

# Last Christmas

*Written and Composed by*
*George Michael*
*In 1984*

Last Christmas I gave you my heart
But the very next day you gave it away
This year, to save me from tears
I'll give it to someone special

Last Christmas I gave you my heart
But the very next day you gave it away
This year, to save me from tears
I'll give it to someone special

Once bitten and twice shy
I keep my distance, but you still catch my eye
Tell me baby, do you recognize me?
Well, it's been a year, it doesn't surprise me

Happy Christmas, I wrapped it up and sent it
With a note saying "I love you", I meant it
Now I know what a fool I've been
But if you kissed me now, I know you'd fool me again

Last Christmas I gave you my heart
But the very next day you gave it away
This year, to save me from tears
I'll give it to someone special

Last Christmas I gave you my heart
But the very next day you gave it away
This year, to save me from tears
I'll give it to someone special

(Continues on next page)

Ooh
Oh, oh, baby

A crowded room, friends with tired eyes
I'm hiding from you and your soul of ice
My God, I thought you were someone to rely on
Me? I guess I was a shoulder to cry on

A face on a lover with a fire in his heart
A man under cover, but you tore me apart
Oh, oh now I've found a real love
You'll never fool me again

Last Christmas I gave you my heart
But the very next day you gave it away
This year, to save me from tears
I'll give it to someone special, special

Last Christmas I gave you my heart
But the very next day you gave it away
This year, to save me from tears
I'll give it to someone special

Special

A face on a lover with a fire in his heart (I gave you mine)
A man under cover but you tore him apart
Maybe next year I'll give it to someone
I'll give it to someone special

Special
So long

Made in the USA
Las Vegas, NV
26 November 2023